VJ DAY
in Photographs

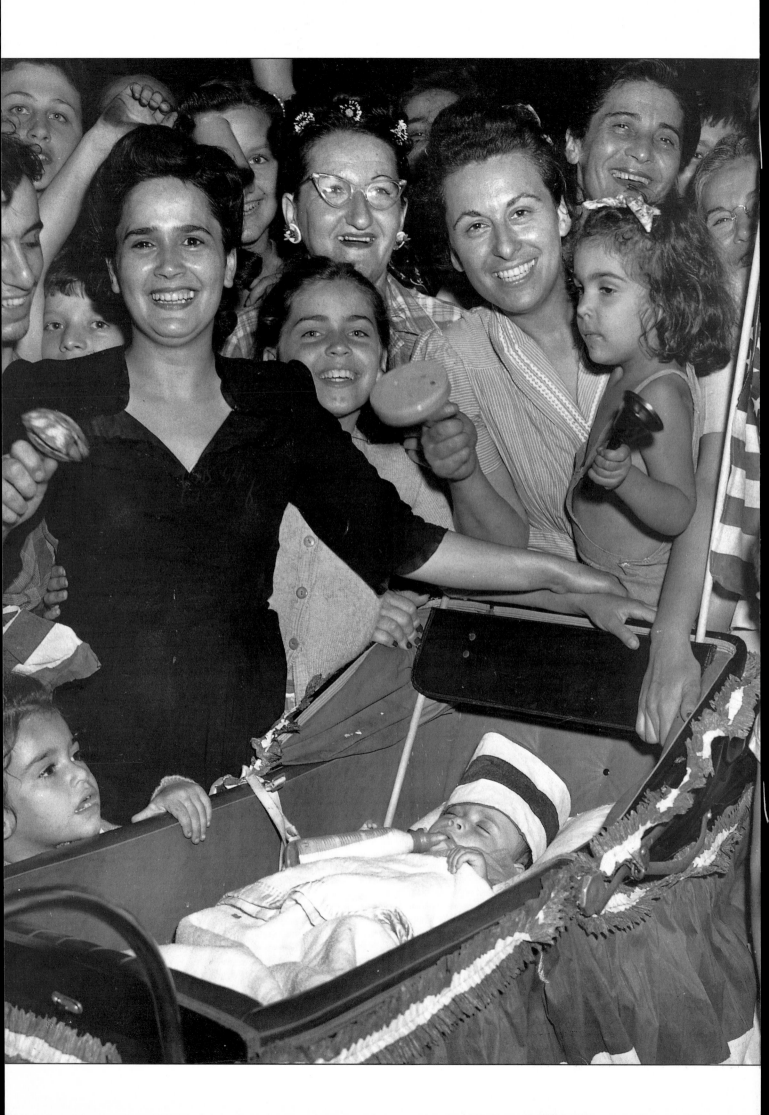

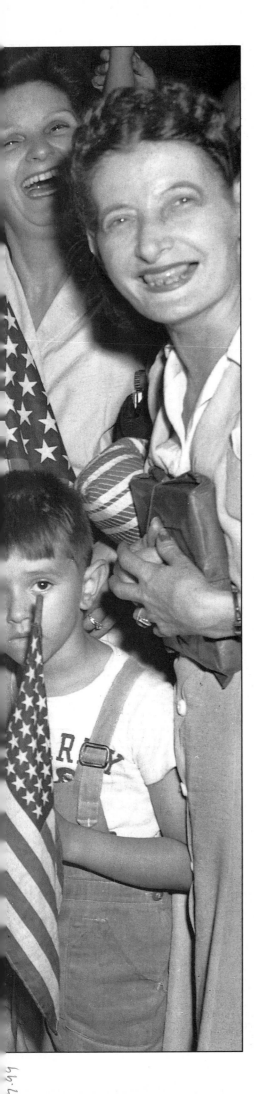

VJ DAY
in Photographs

Edited by Christopher Westhorp

a Salamander book

Published by Salamander Books Limited
LONDON

A SALAMANDER BOOK

Distributed by Random House Value
Publishing, Inc.
40 Engelhard Avenue
Avenel, New Jersey 07001

A CIP catalog record for this book is
available from the Library of Congress.

Printed in Belgium

CREDITS

Designers: John Heritage and Paul Johnson
Text: Christopher Westhorp
Statistics: Compiled by Sean McKnight
Filmset: SX Composing Ltd, England
Color reproduction: P&W Graphics PTE Ltd,
Singapore

9 8 7 6 5 4 3 2 1

940.54g
Wes g

PICTURE CREDITS

The publishers would like to thank Lisa
Leudtke in Washington D.C. for her picture
research and to the following sources for
permission to publish their images. Front
Cover: US National Archives (NA) 80-
G-421127; Back Cover: (top) US Army Signal
Corps (USASC) 415501, (center) USASC
329459, (bottom) Popperfoto; Page 1:
Baltimore Sun; 2/3: Range/Bettmann/UPI
(RBUPI); 4: Imperial War Museum (IWM)
EA75894; 5: Australian War Memorial
(AWM) UK03147; 6/7: Popperfoto; 8: (top)
USAF KKE6014, (bottom) NA 80-G-490421; 9:
(top) NA 80-G-473733, (bottom) NA 49-5278;
10: (top) MacArthur Memorial Archives
(MMA), (bottom) Associated Press (AP); 11:
(top) NA 80-G-354253, (bottom) RBUPI; 12:
(top) Popperfoto, (bottom) IWM EA75898; 13:
(top) IWM EA75901, (bottom) MMA; 14: (top)
Popperfoto, (bottom) IWM D25640; 15: (top)
RBUPI, (bottom) IWM EA75896; 16/17: US
Naval Historical Center (NHC) NH 62594; 18:
(top) RBUPI, (bottom) Harris & Ewing Photo,
courtesy D.C. Public Library; 19: (top) NA 80-
G-490320, (bottom) National Park Services –
Abbie Rowe, courtesy Harry S. Truman
Library, neg 73-2016; 20: (both) RBUPI; 21:
AP; 22: RBUPI; 23: (both) MMA; 24/25: (all)
RBUPI; 26/27: (all) RBUPI; 28: (top) NA 80-
G-338470; (bottom) San Francisco Public
Library (SFPL); 29: (left) MMA, (right) SFPL;
30: (both) Popperfoto; 31: (top) Popperfoto,
(bottom) The Illustrated London News
Picture Library (ILN); 32/33: (all) Popperfoto;
34/35: (all) Popperfoto; 36: (top) Popperfoto,
(bottom) IWM KY77561; 37: (top) ILN,
(bottom) AWM UK03150; 38: (top) IWM
NYP77072, (bottom) RBUPI; 39: (top) AP,
(bottom) RBUPI; 40: (top) AWM 113723,
(bottom) AWM 113026; 41: (top) ILN, (bottom)
AWM 113741; 42/43: NHC NH 33249; 44:
(top) NA 80-G-421130, (bottom) USASC
210644; 45: (top) United States Marine Corps
134711-A, (bottom) MMA; 46: (top) IWM
SE4707, (bottom) NHC NH58261; 47: (top)
Popperfoto, (center) USASC 454970, (bottom)
NA 80-G-707344; 48/49: Popperfoto; 50: NA
80-G-490445; 51: (top) AWM 019146, (bottom)
NA 80-G-473731; 52: (top) USASC 215507,
(bottom) AWM 123732; 53: (top) NA 80-
G-473762, (bottom) AWM 042776; 54/55:
RBUPI; 56: (top) NA 80-G-42118, (bottom) NA
80-G-473728; 57: (top) Popperfoto, (bottom)
RBUPI; 58: (top) NHC NH96187, (bottom) NA
80-G-490440; 59: (both) MMA; 60/61/62 (all)
Popperfoto; 63: (top) IWM SE5011, (bottom)
Popperfoto; 64: Popperfoto.

COVER AND PRELIM IMAGES:

Front Cover: Allied PoWs cheer their
liberators as the first Allied forces move in to
occupy Japan. The men seen here include
Americans, Britons, and Dutchmen.
Back Cover: (top) Early risers in Honolulu on
10 August rejoice upon reading the news;
(center) New Yorkers celebrate VJ Day, 15
August, with tickertape and paper; (bottom)
East Londoners stage a street party.
Page 1: A happy crowd of civilians in
Baltimore, Maryland, wave their copies of the
Baltimore Sun aloft. Pages 2/3: More than
60,000 people celebrated in New York's
Chinatown, but the noise failed to rouse Bobby
DeMarco. Page 4: An impromptu 10 August
victory march on Downing Street, London.
Page 5: St Paul's Cathedral, City of London,
illuminated in all its glory on VJ night.

Contents

Chapter 1

IS IT OVER?

On the morning of 10 August, just one day after the second atomic bomb was dropped, news swept the Allied countries of Japan's acceptance of the surrender terms. Crowds of jubilant servicemen, servicewomen and civilians quickly took to the streets, spreading the news and staging impromptu celebrations. This was one of the scenes in London: a young woman is wearing a copy of the *Evening News* bearing the headline 'JAPAN SURRENDERS' and displaying it to a happy crowd, many of whom are American servicemen. Unfortunately, the news was premature and a tense few days ensued, with several more 'false alarms'.

Indications of the way events were moving had first surfaced on 9 August when Japan's Domei news agency reported that the country's totalitarian party was meeting to discuss 'the sudden development in the war situation'. The Japanese Supreme Council for the Conduct of the War was split on whether to surrender unconditionally or not. The news of 10 August was based on a conditional offer which had been made to the Allies via the Swiss and Swedish, and to this the Allies broadcast a response to Japan on 11 August.

Above and right: The devastating atomic bombing of the seaport of Nagasaki on 9 August inflicted 35,000 immediate dead and provided Japan's leaders with a stark reminder of what lay in store for their country should they continue to resist. The awesome power of 'Fat Boy', a plutonium bomb, suggested dire repercussions. Three million leaflets were dropped on other cities after the bombing, warning of the consequences of Japan's failure to accept unconditional surrender. The next day a further bomb was readied for action.

The new technology involved in this weapon, and the horrendous unlimited power it hinted at, was probably of greater psychological impact than anything else. In terms of destruction and death, conventional bombing attacks were capable of inflicting casualties just as great, and they continued until 15 August. As in Germany, incendiary raids could be terrible, their effect magnified because of the largely wooden construction of Japan's towns and cities. One raid on Tokyo (right) in March had killed 80,000.

Left and below: On 6 August Hiroshima had become the first city ever to be bombed atomically. The uranium bomb 'Little Boy' was used, detonating 2,000ft above the city and flattening 42 sq miles of it – more than half. Some 80,000 people were killed outright (one-third of the population) and tens of thousands injured. The effects of radioactivity were, of course, to follow. The sole Japanese soldiers pictured here merely serve to emphasize the resultant wasteland.

Left: As rumors of surrender abounded, journalists seized on every morsel of information. This is the chaotic scene in the White House Press Office as reporters try to get official confirmation. At one stage President Truman left in a car and the word went around that it was a repeat of the day of Germany's surrender. In fact, the President had merely gone to pick his wife up at the railway station.

Below left: The Federal Communications Commission confirmed the Domei broadcast: Japan would surrender unconditionally if the Emperor could retain his prerogatives. Despite the attempt at a condition the Allied public welcomed the news, as shown by the faces of these servicemen and civilians in Times Square, New York.

Right: Reports quickly reached Alaska where these Soviet and American sailors shared a toast to victory. The Soviet Union had not been at war with Japan until 9 August when their armies crossed the Manchurian frontier in a blitzkrieg advance. This, perhaps more than the atom bombs, precipitated Japan's collapse. By 22 August the Kwantung Army had surrendered.

Below: Thousands of American soldiers, meanwhile, were stationed in Europe securing the peace, and these delirious GIs were photographed in Paris after the news broke. They are probably outside the Rainbow Corner Red Cross Club, a popular hangout there for American servicemen.

Left: London went wild with joy when reports of the surrender went around on 10 August. A delighted American soldier, Sgt. Franklin Talley, sits astride the traffic lights at one of the busiest and most famous intersections in the city, Piccadilly Circus. At one point he shared the position with an equally happy RAF man. He holds aloft the headline that the Allied world had been waiting for. Other servicemen scaled lampposts to affix flags.

Below: London's West End quickly became the scene of spontaneous celebratory street dancing with American service personnel and British civilians participating together eagerly watched by crowds of hundreds while the traffic tried to continue as normal. A traffic policeman who tried to get things moving was carried away shoulder-high in triumph by Allied servicemen, to the crowd's, and his, amusement.

Right: China had been at war with Japan since July 1937 with grave loss of life and untold suffering; tension having simmered since Japan's takeover of Manchuria in 1932. Allied personnel hoisted this Chinese soldier shoulder-high in Piccadilly Circus as their way of marking China's contribution to the Allied victory.

Below: The Japanese Empire covered most of the Far East and therefore many countries and territories had reason to welcome the Japanese defeat. The electric news sparked a gala celebration in Manila in the Philippines on the night of 10 August (actual VJ Day occurred in late September), lasting well into the night. This crowded truck is racing through the streets on a victory tour; any American servicemen became a particular focus of adulation. The man at lower right may well have celebrated too much already! The Philippinos had suffered greatly, the liberation of Manila alone costing 100,000 civilian lives.

Left: Office workers in London's Lower Regent Street, Strand and Aldwych (sites of Australia House and India House respectively) reacted to the news in New York fashion by throwing torn paper and tickertape into the street like confetti. This was the scene in Aldwych on the afternoon of 10 August with the streets ankle-deep and the trees like Christmas trees. The advertisement stating 'For your throat's sake smoke' is a telling sign of the times.

Below left: Downing Street released official news of Japan's negotiations during the early afternoon of 10 August, with a warning to treat it with reserve. It served merely to confirm the rumors and increased the crowds. This New Zealand sailor walking along London's Strand has been joined by English girls and American GIs.

Right and below: Busy enough normally, Piccadilly Circus is the hub between, among others, Regent Street, Piccadilly and Shaftesbury Avenue, and on the afternoon of 10 August the scene was nothing short of chaotic, the vast crowds (below) bringing traffic to a standstill. The statue of Eros had long been covered for wartime protection but it remained a focal point and became the center of celebrations in the West End on that Friday night. These GIs (right) are whooping it up, appropriately, at Eros, Greek god of love. Traffic was eventually diverted and the crowds – and diversions – lasted the weekend.

Chapter 2

VICTORY DAY

Japan eventually declared an official end to hostilities on 14 August, finally accepting the Allies Potsdam ultimatum which had been issued on 26 July. The first official day without war and VJ Day, for Victory over Japan, was the next day, 15 August. The US Fleet at harbor in Leyte Gulf in the Philippines (right) celebrated the news, courtesy of Fleet Adm. Nimitz, by firing off pyrotechnic flares and illuminating the night sky in a victory firework show. The scene was repeated in other US naval bases at Pearl Harbor and elsewhere.

Above and left: Citizens gathered in Washington D.C. from the early hours of 14 August awaiting official news. Military Policemen set up barricades (left) in front of the White House and State Department in order to control the anticipated crowds. These women naval personnel, or WAVES, are being directed away from the area. Many people gathered in nearby Lafayette Park, indulging in party atmosphere snake dances (above) until the evening proclamation.

Above right: For Japanese the act of surrender was humiliation. These Prisoners of War (PoWs) on Guam are listening, heads bowed, to Emperor Hirihito's announcement in the late morning (Tokyo time) of 15 August as the last air raid on Tokyo was in progress. Weeping crowds stood outside the Imperial Palace, 30 of whom committed suicide after the news. The very fact of hearing the Emperor was almost as shocking as the content, being the first time the public had ever heard his voice. On 18 August a new Japanese cabinet was sworn in under Prince Higashi-Kuni who ordered the army to obey the Emperor and lay down their arms.

Right: The historic moment as President Harry S. Truman made the official announcement of Japan's unconditional surrender to assembled journalists on 14 August at 7pm local time. Truman stated that VJ Day should await the formal surrender signing but White House officials quickly released details afterwards of a two-day declaration of holiday for federal employees on the 15th and 16th.

Above: Official news of victory brought thousands of people onto the streets of New York. These servicemen, marching line abreast through Times Square, had waited all day for the news. New York's Mayor La Guardia made an emotional broadcast to the populace, invoking the memory of Franklin Delano Roosevelt.

Below: Monitors had picked up reports during the early hours, so it was a long day until the surrender became official. These sailors in New York are clearly delighted; others were thankful and hundreds knelt in prayer outside a full St Patrick's Cathedral.

Right: Unrestrained joy shows on the faces of these citizens of Oak Ridge, Tennessee, assembled in the town's Jackson Square holding aloft copies of *The Knoxville Journal*. Known as 'the secret city', Oak Ridge supplied the enriched uranium for the Hiroshima bomb and plutonium-processing research for the Nagasaki one. The people here had therefore made a special contribution to the Allied victory.

Left: Joy was unconfined in New York's Little Italy when news broke on 14 August. The district was proud of its enthusiasm and vociferousness and demonstrates it here all too clearly. Greenwich Village, Queens, the Bronx, Brooklyn, Staten Island and other districts all went crazy too!

Right: New York's Garment District near Penn Station was quick to show its feelings with great showers of tickertape and confetti to augur in the VJ party. Thousands of workers took to the streets in an event to remember for a lifetime. In the space of 24 hours New York's Sanitation Department cleared 4,863 tons of paper – more than double the previous record.

Below: The citizens of Gotham on the East Side were on the streets before dawn on 14 August, prior to the official announcements. Drums, flags and street decorations had all been readied for the moment weeks beforehand.

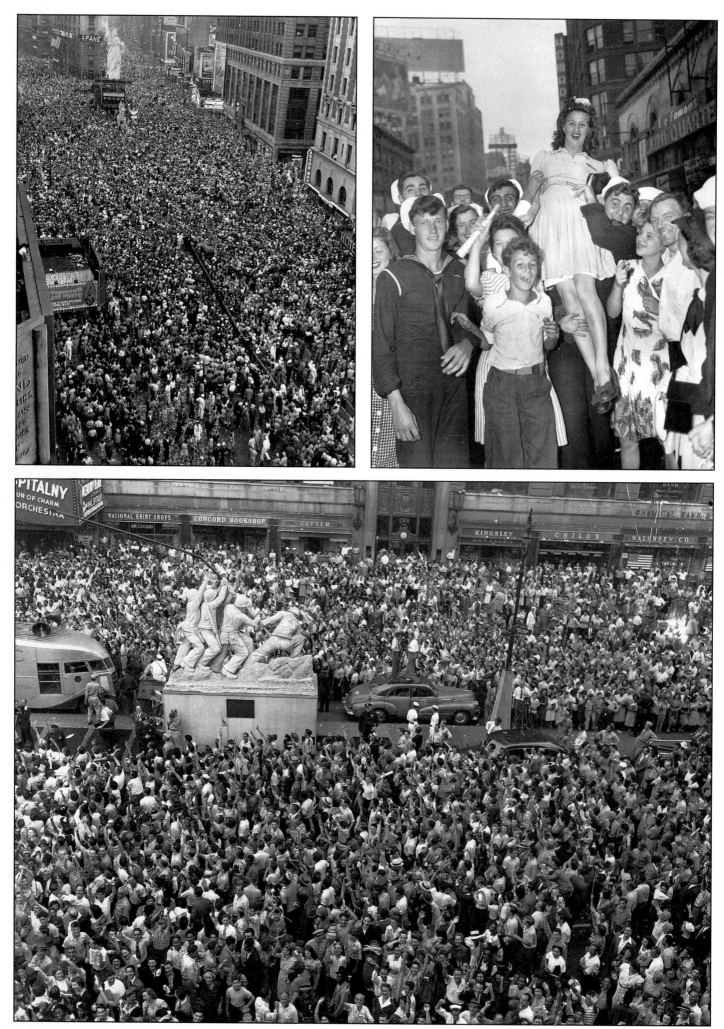

It was estimated that in the New York metropolitan area some eight million people joined in the noisy celebrations on VJ Day which marked the end of World War II and became possibly the greatest event in the city's history. In Times Square an electric sign lit up at 7:03pm with the message: 'Official: Truman announces Japanese surrender'. The resultant din was deafening as factory and ships' sirens sounded, people cheered and car horns honked.

Far left: A tremendous crowd fill Times Square; this view, looking south, shows the replica of the Statue of Liberty which had been erected to boost sales of war bonds (the electric signboard is behind it). About 500,000 had gathered for the official announcement which they greeted with a mighty roar, repeated for 20 minutes. Strangers embraced and noise was made with every device imaginable. By 10pm Chief Inspector John J. O'Connell estimated there were two million people in the area – an all-time record – and packed so tightly that the crowd was almost one entity. Still people continued to pour into the area by subway, buses and foot.

Left: Jubilant sailors hoist aloft a girl in Times Square. Big crowds remained in Times Square until well after midnight. At 3am some 500,000 were still in party mood and many remained for all of the next day too. Things remained good natured throughout.

Below left: The crowd fills the area of Times Square opposite the Statue of Liberty, the section around the symbolic backdrop provided by the momentous flag raising at Mount Suribachi on Iwo Jima, an iconographic moment of American military prowess in the Pacific photographed by Joe Rosenthal.

Right: Merchant Seaman Alex Caperna of Baltimore clambered up this lamppost in the center of Times Square to lash Old Glory to the mast during the height of the victory celebration. The enormous crowd loved it and cheered him loudly.

Left: A sailor provides his own personal victory salute to his girlfriend outside the Trans-Lux Theater in Times Square. Many people were actually in movie theaters when the news broke in mid-performance. In Radio City Music Hall the news was flashed onto the screen and the audience of 6,000 rose from their seats and cheered.

Right: For some it was a very long day of festivities. This sailor, merchant marine pilot and their girlfriends, however, are still seeking out even more along the Great White Way on VJ Day night.

Below: War is over! And for many the best thing was to find a partner and attempt to dance an old-fashioned round dance in the open but busy spaces of Times Square.

Left: For those still in the Pacific Theater of Operations, VJ Day meant much more to them than civilians, comfortable and safe at home, could ever realize. These men of 22nd Special Naval Construction Battalion are celebrating with gusto at their naval amphibious base at Manus in the Admiralty Islands. For them the end of war signalled an imminent prospect of home, hence the sign: 'Goodbye Pacific – Hello USA'.

Right: People took to the streets throughout the United States, not just in New York and Washington D.C., but in many other towns and cities too, large and small. These two women, Sue Davis and Elizabeth Lennox, are cheering themselves hoarse from the window of Detroit City Hall during the early hours. One over-enthusiastic celebrant has found his own peace, sleeping things off on the ledge below them. A scene no doubt repeated in countless places elsewhere.

Above and left: The scene on VJ Day in Market Street, San Francisco, was boisterous, with thousands of sailors filling the city who then proceeded to light bonfires in the street and dance atop vehicles, grabbing the local ladies for victory embraces. As the day wore on things got out of hand and windows were broken, shops looted and the State Riot Act eventually read. It took 1,000 police and naval shore patrolmen to disperse a mob consisting mainly of sailors. Sadly, several people were killed and hundreds injured.

Left: After London's popular celebrations of 10, 11 and 12 August it was a surprise that many still had the energy left for VJ Day itself when it came on 15 August. Most of the dancers seen here in Regent Street are women despite the fact that there appear to be young men in the crowd of onlookers.

Below: Many British men were, of course, in the forces, a fact made apparent by this Cockney street celebration along Fleet Street, then home of Britain's newspaper industry. Many of those surrounding the accordion player are too old or young to have served in the forces.

Right and below right: The Metropolitan Police Band provided the musical entertainment on VJ Day in Trafalgar Square for a crowd of 100,000 (right), while in Piccadilly Circus (below right) a huge audience listened to a band playing on the balcony of the US Rainbow Club in nearby Shaftesbury Avenue. The band was The Mustangs of 361st Fighter Group. The club was the central West End focus for American servicemen and was hosting a victory dance.

Left and above: The official announcement
from Prime Minister Clement Attlee came at
midnight on 14/15 August and a two-day
holiday was announced. The partying began
immediately and people flooded into central
London to join in. (It was still going strong
into 16 August in London's West End.)
Revellers lit bonfires in the street around
which they danced and sang patriotic
wartime songs; the scene at left took place in
Piccadilly, closed once again to traffic by
sheer force of numbers. Women were tossed
from blankets into the air; barrel organs
provided music for all-night singing and
dancing; and those unable or unwilling to
return home just slept in the streets.

Left: Crowds in party mood, with the burden
of six years of war lifted, meant an
opportunity to sell and London's market
traders were not slow to seize it. During the
war, and for years after, food was rationed,
but in the Strand at midnight people queued
eagerly for fruit. People wanting bread were
not as fortunate.

Right: Auxiliary Territorial Service (ATS)
girls, having made their contribution, reap
the rewards of victory night in scenes
repeated throughout the United Kingdom in
villages, towns and big cities as the country
indulged in a massive party.

Left: The morning after the night before and it is time to clear up in Piccadilly after the all-night party. The débris of hats, streamers and newspapers, not to mention beer bottles and broken chairs, began to get cleared up before the crowds had dispersed.

Below and right: Party hats, flags and bunting provide the essential ingredients for the street party, a traditionally British way of celebrating in tight-knit communities. Both these street scenes are in London just after VJ Day: Battersea's Ascalon Street to the south of the River Thames and Lowell Street, Limehouse, in the bomb-blighted docklands to the east. Plenty of women and children but few men suggests most had yet to return to their families, although it must have been imminent (note Ascalon Street's 'Welcome Home' sign).

Below right: Not even born when the war broke out, this little girl will remember Lowell Street's party because it was probably her first experience of the treats and cakes loved by children everywhere. Note the V for Victory atop the table.

Left and below: Buckingham Palace and its environs are a traditional gathering point for crowds during national occasions and the end of World War II was no exception. As ever at the big event some seek out the best vantage points and invariably the schoolboys prove themselves to be the most adept climbers of all, occupying nearly all the positions atop this monument. Prime Minister Clement Attlee went to the palace on 14 August in order to be received by King George VI and the crowd had gathered at the Victoria Monument at the front (below) and nearby areas in order to catch a glimpse of the new Labour Prime Minister and perhaps the royal family. The visit signalled to the country that an official announcement was imminent.

Right: VJ Day in London was the occasion for the State Opening of Parliament and despite the rainy weather the crowds turned out in their thousands to watch the return of the King and Queen from their trip to Westminster. That night at 9pm the King broadcast to the nation via the BBC. The speech was also relayed by loudspeakers to a massive crowd outside the palace. The royal family made a total of six balcony appearances to take the salute of the crowd during the course of the day, the last at midnight with the Queen resplendent in a diamond tiara under the floodlights. Even the princesses had joined the crowd to watch the final appearance.

Below: Buckingham Palace was illuminated on VJ night (as were other major sights) to mark the Allied and Empire victory. Although the war in the Far East was not a direct experience for many, unless they had relatives fighting or imprisoned there, the defeat of Japan meant that war was at last over, and Londoners and other Britons who had suffered greatly during the Blitz felt they fully deserved their second big day of victory. A national day of thanksgiving and prayer for victory was scheduled for Sunday 19 August.

AWM UK 03150

Above left: For others, the war in the Far East had been an all too direct experience. This was the scene in Shanghai, one of China's major ports and cities, in late-August as the people celebrated the defeat of the Japanese Empire after a brutal occupation that left millions dead. Kuomintang troops had liberated the city on 25 August but large Communist forces were ominously close. Talks between the rival sides had stalemated.

Left: Normally a reserved people, the joy occasioned by the end of the war led to tumultuous scenes such as that photographed here in Chungking as thousands of Chinese took to the streets eager to celebrate and think hopefully of the future. Marshal Chiang Kai-shek announced to the people: 'Our faith in justice through the black and hopeless days of eight long years of struggle has been rewarded.' Unfortunately, more years of privation and war lay ahead, this time of civil war.

Above and right: Many Chinese lived abroad and these were scenes in New York's Chinatown a couple of weeks earlier. These Chinese sailors and cymbal players (above) entertaining bystanders were reacting to the false reports of surrender on 12 August that were later withdrawn in error. Two days later, on the evening of 14 August, and the news was official and Chinatown hosted the largest crowd in its history outnumbering the resident population 10 to one; this man and his son (right) cross their Stars and Stripes in a V for Victory. Four ritualistic dragons led the parades as gongs sounded and firecrackers exploded.

Left: Australia and New Zealand made a mighty contribution to Japan's defeat. These hastily improvised signs mark Victory in the Pacific Day (as it is known in Australia) for these Australians of 7th Division in the Balikpapan area of Borneo. The Borneo campaign had been bitterly fought and Japan was all but defeated by the time of the Balikpapan landings in July which many considered wasteful of Australian manpower and lives so late in the war. The looks of delight on the faces of these soldiers reveal a relief that their sacrifices are over at last.

Below left: Australians were informed of the surrender at 9am on 14 August by their Prime Minister Ben Chifley and two days of holiday were declared: the 15th for rejoicing and the 16th for marches. Happy crowds gathered in the towns and cities of Australia on VP Day, and this was the scene in Bourke Street, Melbourne, on 15 August. On 24 August there was a large Combined Services Victory March down the same street.

Right: An aerial view of the large crowd at the thanksgiving service held at Melbourne's Shrine of Remembrance on 16 August. All Australian State capitals held similar multi-denominational events combined with parades. Canberra's was held at the Australian War Memorial.

Below: On 16 August Sydney hosted an upbeat Combined Services Victory March through the city's streets led by Victoria Cross holder Sgt. R. Rattey; in addition a crowd of several hundred thousand attended this more reflective service in the city's Hyde Park afterwards. Those attending either or both were not just Pacific veterans, but Australians who had fought with great distinction in North Africa and the Middle East. Over 600,000 men had gone into uniform and 17,500 died in the Pacific alone, nearly half of them in Japanese camps.

Chapter 3

SURRENDER

Japan having accepted the terms of surrender on 14 August, the official surrender ceremony was scheduled for 2 September aboard the American warship USS *Missouri* at anchor in Tokyo Bay. On the appointed day the 11-man Japanese delegation arrived at 8:30am for the proceedings presided over by Gen. MacArthur as the Supreme Commander of the Allied Powers. Other signatories attended from the USA, Britain, China, Australia, the Netherlands, New Zealand, the Soviet Union, France and Canada. The Japanese delegation's signatories were their new foreign minister, Mamoru Shigemitsu, and Gen. Yoshijiro Umezu (at front right and left respectively in the photograph). The ceremony only lasted 20 minutes. A flurry of other surrenders followed: 6 September, Rabaul; 8 September Bougainville; 9 September, Nanking; 11 September, Timor and Rangoon; 12 September, Singapore; 13 September, New Guinea; and 16 September, Hong Kong. After accepting the signed surrender document Gen. MacArthur said, 'Let us pray that peace be now restored to the world and that God will preserve it always. These proceedings are closed.'

Above: One of the key elements contributing to the Allied victory was superior air power and the surrender ceremony of 2 September seemed an appropriate moment to make that point. More than a thousand planes flew over the American and British warships. Those pictured here are US Navy carrier planes such as the TBM Avenger, F6F Hellcat, SB2C Helldiver and F4U Corsair. The B-29 Superfortress, in particular, played a crucial role in the bombardment of Japan, making over 34,000 sorties including the atomic missions, and 400 circled overhead on the day.

Left: Naturally, many people were keen to witness the historic moment of surrender. This picture shows the crush for a vantage point. As a symbolic presence, the United States flew the Perry Flag from the Memorial Hall of the US Naval Academy at Annapolis, Maryland, and put it near the spot for the signing (bottom right of picture). This flag (with just 30 stars for states) was that hoisted by M. C. Perry on 14 July 1853 in Tokyo Bay on his expedition to negotiate the first treaty between Japan and the United States.

Right, above: The moment when Gen. Douglas MacArthur signed the document. Behind him are Lt. Gen. J. Wainwright (left), who surrendered after Bataan and Corregidor, and Lt. Gen. A. E. Percival, the British commander who surrendered at Singapore. Both had just been liberated two weeks earlier after years of captivity.

Right: The document was afterwards entrusted to Col. Bernard Thielen and flown to Washington D.C. where, on 7 September, he handed it to President Truman in the Oval Office at the White House.

Left: Gen. Itagaki signs the surrender document for the Japanese forces in Malaysia on 12 September in the Municipal Buildings, Singapore. Adm. Lord Mountbatten, signatory for the Allies, watches from the desk opposite. It was a satisfying moment for the British, for the fall of 'Fortress Singapore' in February 1942, with 130,000 men captured, had been the nadir of their fortunes in the Far East.

Below: The war in the Pacific had been a particularly triumphant moment for the US Navy. Therefore in October the return of Fleet Adm. Chester W. Nimitz to Washington D.C. had all the sense of a Roman commander's victory triumph in Ancient Rome. Here he is seen taking the salute of the admiring crowd from his open car. Sat at his right is Rear Adm. Forrest Sherman, to his left is his aide, Cdr. H. A. Lamar.

Right, top: The Sino-Japanese War ended with the main Japanese surrender, but until then the Japanese had been fighting and capitulating to two different Chinese armies, the Nationalist and the Communist. The surrender pictured here in Nanking on 9 September was to Chiang Kai-shek's Kuomintang nationalists. It marked an end to one set of hostilities and the beginning of another, for China was a country divided.

Right, center: Long dominated by the Japanese, the Korean peninsula was liberated by the Allies and given independence. This picture was taken on 10 September 1945 and shows US Army troops of 32nd Infantry, 7th Division, standing at rest as the Japanese flag is lowered.

Right, bottom: The crew and midshipmen of USS *Missouri* celebrate the fourth anniversary of VJ Day during the Naval Academy's midshipmen's cruise by gathering around the plaque marking the spot where Japan surrendered on 2 September 1945.

Chapter 4

GOING HOME

Hundreds of thousands of Allied prisoners, both military and civilian, were held in PoW and civilian internment camps located across Japanese-occupied East Asia and Japan proper. These elated Allied prisoners (right) have been liberated after years of incarceration at the notorious Changi Prison, Singapore. These few hundred men are just a fraction of the 6,000 inmates, many of whom had been there for over three years, since the fall of Singapore.

As well as the inhuman, unsanitary conditions, the prisoners were deliberately malnourished and treated in a brutal fashion with complete disregard for international conventions. The Japanese used forced labor – most notoriously on the Burma-Thai railway – and conducted chemical and biological warfare experiments on prisoners in Manchuria, mostly on Chinese. Thousands of prisoners died (the ratio was seven times as high as for Allied PoWs in Europe), many brutally murdered, and those that survived were, for the most part, in a shocking and emaciated condition. Nurses were sent out to assist with the rehabilitation process and in September the first prisoners began to return home to their loved ones.

Above: Many of the prisoners were civilians, but they fared little better in terms of treatment. Most of this group were captured in Rabaul and held at Yokohama. They are pictured here at a PoW processing unit in Manila before they go home. Four are Australian Army nurses, six are civilian nurses from Rabaul Government Hospital, four are nurses from the Methodist Mission, one an American schoolteacher captured in the Aleutian Islands, one a housewife and one a civilian.

Left: Holding aloft an American flag these Allied PoWs at the Aomori Camp, near Yokohama, cheer their US Navy rescuers on 29 August 1945 following the beginning of the occupation of Japan.

Right: These Greek sailors had been held as prisoners in a Franciscan Convent in Saitama Prefecture, 30 miles north of Tokyo, since 1941. The supplies they are holding were dropped by American planes towards the end of August 1945.

乗車口

Above: Recently released American PoWs wave to onlookers as they leave the railroad station in Yokohama on 20 September 1945. The first stop for many was Hawaii.

Left: Sapper Tiddes of Australia's 9th Division Engineers waves a bandaged arm to friends from one of the lower portholes of the hospital ship *Wanganella* as it arrives at Circular Quay, Sydney, from New Guinea carrying long-service men and women returning home on 23 November 1945. Australian demobilization was well organized via a discharge depot and the civil reestablishment wing which provided the soldier with the means to reintegrate: an identity card, food coupon book, clothing coupons, and a tobacco permit.

AWM 123732

Right: Discharged Japanese soldiers and sailors crowd a railway car at Hiroshima, taking advantage of free transport home in September 1945. Note the navy's anchor insignia emblazoned on some caps and the army's star on others.

Below: These pensive faces of Australian womanhood belong not to widows but to GI brides and fiancées. With victory won, these women are preparing to leave for the United States to begin married life with the servicemen they have met during their wartime stationing in Australia. Here, the women are attending a lecture intended to educate them on what lies in store for them in a new life abroad. In August 1945 it was estimated that 10,000 Australians would eventually go to the United States.

AWM 042776

Chapter 5

THE LONG WAY BACK

The Allied occupation of Japan began on 27 August 1945 when, at 5:30am GMT, 112 Allied warships sailed into anchorage in Sagami Bay, just outside the entrance to Tokyo Bay. Four days later MacArthur established the Allied HQ at Yokohama. The Allies were to remain until 1952.

For both the occupiers and occupied it was a tremendous culture shock, very few people at the time having encountered much in the way of foreign lands and new cultures and customs. To the surprise of many, things went exceedingly smoothly.

A traditional feature of Japanese society were the geisha girls. Open to potential misinterpretation by westerners, the geishas were legitimate entertainers trained in singing, dancing, musical instruments and conversation. The Allied servicemen quickly appreciated them and their teahouses; and the geishas were quick to welcome them, with signs appearing in English and urging them to visit. Here, American servicemen share a beer with some waitresses at the Recreation Amusement Association Club in the Ginza district of Tokyo.

Above: US Marines going ashore for the initial occupation near Yokosuka on the morning of 28 August 1945; units of 11th Airborne Division landed at Atsugi airfield. These were the forerunners; the occupation began in strength the next day.

Left: Seaman Paul Gray from San Dimos, California, practices riding a Japanese bicycle while carrying a traditional umbrella as a parasol in late-August 1945.

Above right: Beau and Kay Glendining, sisters serving with the Women's Auxiliary Service (WAS) of the British Occupation Force in Japan, being greeted in customary Japanese tradition by the Japanese house girls who would bring flowers and bow every morning they arrived for work. The British forces employed many Japanese as waitresses, teachers, and so on.

Right: American relations with the Japanese were soon cordial thanks to restraint and understanding. Punishment was swift for those obstructing the military occupiers, but was equally as harsh for Allied troops that abused their position. Here, the United States makes an early cultural export of the jitterbug as Cpl. Stanley Suski of Reading, Pennsylvania, whirls Miss Tamako, a geisha. Ironically, one thing which didn't need to be exported was baseball, the Japanese having played it since 1869.

One of the tasks of the occupying forces was to destroy Japan's capacity to wage aggressive war again. A new constitution was drafted by the Allies, approved in Japan's 1946 elections and introduced in 1947. Among other things, it sought to curb militarism in the future and to establish a constitutional monarchy. Initially, however, the problem was to destroy the weaponry that already existed, much of which was highly unsafe. The British found more than 30,000 tons of ammunition and explosives in just one network of caves at Kure – all of which was unprotected.

Left: The Japanese Navy was particularly large and had to be dismantled or converted. Here, the Japanese Tachibana class escort destroyer *Odake* is converted for repatriation service at Maizuru Navy Yard in October 1945.

Below: Immediately after the occupation had begun, this US Marine was set to work breaking Japanese small arms at Futtsusaki Point, near Yokosuka Naval Base. Japanese soldiers staged farewell parades, handed in their weapons at collection centers and then demobilized back into civilian life.

Above: Occupation was not just about destruction of arms, it was also about reconstruction of the Japanese economy and society. The process was not an overnight one, but over time, in both Japan and Germany, it can safely be said that the United States did a quite remarkable job. The Allies quickly put the Japanese to work rebuilding their shattered country; here a new garden takes root in the midst of the rubble and bomb damage.

Right: In the Allied commander, MacArthur, the Japanese found for themselves a new shogun. Introducing multiple reforms of land, suffrage, trade unions, and so on, he gained a large following in the country. He was urged to run for the US Presidency, but he never did. This popularity deluded him; he disobeyed Truman on numerous occasions and was eventually recalled to the United States in 1951. The Japanese – even the Emperor – were devastated to see him go.

Chapter 6

UNFINISHED BUSINESS

The restoration of peace was also a time for the settlement of accounts with those who had begun the war and committed unspeakable crimes against humanity. The Allies took the decisioin at Potsdam to hold International War Crimes Tribunals to investigate and punish those responsible. On 8 August the War Crimes Committee reported in London that a new code of international law had been agreed defining aggressive warfare as a crime against the world and providing punishment for those who provoked such war.

The International Military Tribunal for the Far East was set up in January 1946. Its hearings lasted three years, tried thousands of individuals, and were held across the region in places where the Japanese had perpetrated their crimes. The big show trial, however, was in Tokyo. It began in June 1946 and in the dock were 28 Japanese deemed to be their war leaders. It ended in November 1948; two had died (Matsuoka and Adm. Nagano) and one been declared insane (Okawa), seven were hanged, 16 imprisoned for life, and two jailed for shorter terms.

This picture (right) was taken in May when the charges were read. Only 25 men can be seen. From left to right, they are: (back row) Gen. Koiso (life), Adm. Nagano, Gen. Oshima (life), Gen. Matsui (death), Okawa, Hiranuma (life), Togo (20 years), Matsuoka, Shigemitsu (7 years), Gen. Sato (life), Shimada (life), Shiratori (life), and Maj. Gen. Susuki (life); (front row) Gen. Dohihara (death), Kaya (life), Hirota (death), Gen. Minami (life), Gen. Tojo (death), Rear Adm. Oka (life), Gen. Umezu (life), Gen. Araki (life), Gen. Muto (death), Hoshino (life), Hata (life), and Kido (life). Also sentenced were Hashimoto (life), Kimura (death) and Itagaki (death).

Right: Changi Prison, Singapore, was a brutal hellhole in which Allied prisoners were incarcerated in their thousands, many for more than three years. With the war won and the Allied prisoners liberated, it was the turn of the Japanese to be detained on suspicion of war crimes. Maj. Tim Heal, the new military governor of the jail, is being saluted by Lt.Gen. Mutaguchi Renya who had commanded the army that conquered the Malay peninsula and was being held at Changi awaiting trial together with some 700 other Japanese, all put to work making furniture for British Army schools.

Below: When the Japanese seized Singapore they interned policeman P.J.H. Hockenhull in Changi and kept him there for the next three-and-a-half years, during which time his jailor was the brutal guard Tominago. Having survived to be liberated, policeman Hockenhull has the satisfaction of being able to point to his tormentor safely behind bars.

Right: The jails were quickly filled with Japanese after Singapore was restored to British control. Here, Lt. Col. Kazuo Nakamura and 20 other Kempei Tai officials are being marched through the streets to Pearl Jail in September 1945 watched by onlookers. The Kempei Tai were Army Military Police and responsible for many of the most brutal acts committed.

Below: Outram Road Jail, Singapore, was another notorious wartime place of confinement. Its commandant, Koshiro Mikizawa, was suspected of involvement in atrocities and questioned thoroughly by intelligence officers. He eventually admitted to beheadings and took his interrogators to a small clearing in the jungle growth which he identified as the spot where executions had taken place and the victims were buried.

EPILOGUE

The war in Asia had started in China two years before Germany had invaded Poland, and it was the Chinese who suffered the largest number of Asian casualties. Figures for Chinese fatalities vary wildly from 2.5 million to as high as 15 million, and for the Chinese fighting did not finish in 1945; in 1947 a covert civil war raging since 1943 flared into full-blooded war, and within a year of the Chinese Civil War ending "volunteers" from the People's Liberation Army found themselves fighting in the Korean War. Japan, whose attempts to create an East Asian Empire had sparked off the war, suffered more than two million fatalities, and with the demise of their Empire over 7 million Japanese were repatriated back home. Despite the immense human losses in China, the Asian War was lost by the Japanese in the Pacific. Just over 110,000 Americans died defeating Japan, and the nature of war in the Pacific allowed the USA to exploit its industrial strength fully. Between 1941 and 1945 the USA constructed 8.5 million tons of warships and 51 million tons of merchant ships, effectively crushing Japan who had been the worlds third largest naval power in 1941. British and Imperial forces (principally Indian) fought a subsiding but important campaign in Southeast Asia, (the British suffered 250,000 casualties in battle there) and by 1945 had reconquered much of what was lost in 1942.

The war in Asia precipitated massive political change: Japan's intervention in China had weakened the Kuomintang government and made it possible for the Chinese Communists to take power, and in Southeastern Asia the humiliation of the European colonial powers in 1942 was a harbinger of the end of their empires. It was to be in Asia where the new nuclear age was born with such violence over Hiroshima on 6 August 1945, and that the Cold War was to be at its hottest. August 1945, for the East, was a pause in wars rather than a return to peace.